# WORKBOOK AND JOURNAL FOR

# MASTER OF THE PIECES

*Being Restored, Redeemed, and Empowered by the Love of God*

## JOELLE MARYN

# CONTENTS

## APPENDIX

# INTRODUCTION

This workbook is a companion to the *Master of the Pieces* book by Joelle Maryn.

Most of our broken pieces contain identity lies that stand in the way of being who God has called us to be. This workbook will guide you through naming the lies and sharing the truth so that you can move forward in your life's purpose.

Each chapter contains three sections:

- RESTORED—A summary of key healing points from "Master of the Pieces."

- REDEEMED—Identity lies and the Scriptures that go against those lies.

- EMPOWERED—Reflection questions and a prayer.

The Appendix also includes a guide to help you put your story together—because your story is His glory!

It's important not to rush the process. As you go through the chapters, ask the Holy Spirit to bring things to mind to help you with the questions. Then wait patiently for His truth to sink into the deepest recesses of your heart.

This workbook will help you allow the "Master of your pieces" to shine His light in the darkest places to restore, redeem, and empower you to live the life He has planned for you. It's time to let Him break the chains that have been holding you back, so that you can be fully alive in who you've been created to be!

# OPENING PRAYER

*Lord Jesus, please fill me with your Holy Spirit and guide my thoughts and heart as I go through this workbook. Please bring all of my darkness to the light and heal me in any way that is needed: mind, heart, body, and soul. Please restore, redeem, and empower me to do your will. Let me hear you speaking to me and help me know who I truly am so that I may love and serve you better. Amen.*

## CHAPTER 1

# REPENTANCE AND FAITH

## RESTORED

Many times, what the world tells us will make us happy only leaves us emptier inside, and material things can never fill the holes in our hearts. As Saint Augustine said, "You have made us for yourself, O Lord, and our hearts are restless until they rest in You."

We can also get to the point where we look in the mirror and we don't even recognize ourselves anymore—especially when we allow the culture to guide us and get wrapped up in what other people think about us. However, Jesus is our only true judge and what He thinks of us is all that matters. And despite any of the mistakes we've made in our lives, even the ones that have left us feeling completely annihilated and shattered into pieces—God will never give up on us!

Don't forget, He knows your intense longing to be known and loved. He hears your cries and desires to heal you. All is not lost because all is restorable and redeemable.

Let us now dive into the truth and be empowered by His love.

# REDEEMED

## IDENTITY LIES:

- My identity comes from how I look and how others perceive me.
- I'm not chosen.
- The things of the world will satisfy me.

## THE TRUTH:

*Psalm 139:13–14—"You formed my inmost being; you knit me in my mother's womb. I praise you, because I am wonderfully made; wonderful are your works! My very self you know."*

*John 15:16—"It was not you who chose me, but I who chose you and appointed you to go and bear fruit that will remain, so that whatever you ask the Father in my name he may give you."*

*Ephesians 1:11—"In him we were also chosen, destined in accord with the purpose of the One who accomplishes all things according to the intention of his will."*

*1 John 2:16—"For all that is in the world, sensual lust, enticement for the eyes, and a pretentious life, is not from the Father but is from the world."*

*John 14:27—"Peace I leave with you; my peace I give to you. Not as the world gives do I give it to you. Do not let your hearts be troubled or afraid."*

# EMPOWERED

## PICKING UP THE PIECES

Have you ever thought you had it all together and tried to tell God the way you think things should go? Share the experience here.

_______________________________________________

_______________________________________________

_______________________________________________

_______________________________________________

_______________________________________

_______________________________________

_______________________________________

_______________________________________

Have you ever looked in the mirror and felt like what you see doesn't match how you feel on the inside? Explain what you saw and how you felt.

_______________________________________

_______________________________________

_______________________________________

_______________________________________

_______________________________________

_______________________________________

_______________________________________

Are you ready to cry out and open your heart to hear the plans that God has for you? Write an honest plea for help to God sharing your heart and desires.

_______________________________________

_______________________________________

# PRAYER

*Lord Jesus, please help me to know who I am in you, why I am here, and what your plan is for my life. I come to you with an open heart and a desire to hear your voice. Please guide me, strengthen me, and console me. Help me to know, love, and serve you better. Please, Lord, help pick up the pieces. Please restore, redeem, and empower me. Amen.*

## CHAPTER 2

—————————————

# TRUTH AND LOVE

## RESTORED

S in separates us from God and leads to confusion about our identity and purpose. We become more self-centered instead of God-centered. However, God doesn't want us to remain in sin and He gives us light as an act of mercy. He wants us to use the gifts and graces we've been given to help build His kingdom. This will be our ultimate joy.

Remember to live each day like it's your last so that when you face Him at your death, you will have no regrets in this life and will have fulfilled your purpose and mission to love.

As Saint John of the Cross says, "In the evening of life, we will be judged on love alone."

# REDEEMED

## IDENTITY LIES:

- Life is all about me.
- It's not a big deal if I sin.

## THE TRUTH:

*1 Peter 4:8—"Above all, let your love for one another be intense, because love covers a multitude of sins."*

*John 15:12–13—"This is my commandment: love one another as I love you. No one has greater love than this, to lay down one's life for one's friends."*

*Philippians 2:3—"Do nothing out of selfishness or out of vainglory; rather, humbly regard others as more important than yourselves."*

*Galatians 6:9—"Let us not grow tired of doing good, for in due time we shall reap our harvest, if we do not give up."*

*2 Corinthians 5:10—"For we must all appear before the judgment seat of Christ, so that each one may receive recompense, according to what he did in the body, whether good or evil."*

*Psalm 90:12—"Teach us to count our days aright, that we may gain wisdom of heart."*

# EMPOWERED

## PICKING UP THE PIECES

How may you be blinded by sin? What sins do you keep repeating that you have gotten used to? What do you think is the root wound underneath those sins?

_______________________________________________________

_______________________________________________________

_______________________________________________________

_______________________________________________________

_______________________________________________________

_______________________________________________________

_______________________________________________________

Are you aware that God has given you gifts and that you are called to use them to help others?

_______________________________________________

_______________________________________________

_______________________________________________

_______________________________________________

_______________________________________________

_______________________________________________

_______________________________________________

_______________________________________________

How are you filling your good column—the column to love and use the gifts, talents, and graces God gave you to build His kingdom?

_______________________________________________

_______________________________________________

_______________________________________________

_______________________________________________

_______________________________________________

_______________________________________________

_______________________________________________

_______________________________________________

# PRAYER

*Dear Jesus, please give me light to see my sins so that I may truly repent and turn away from all things that offend you. Please help me to see the gifts you've given me and guide me on how to use them to bring you glory. Thank you for your eternal love and mercy. Amen.*

## CHAPTER 3

# GRIEF

## RESTORED

At some point, most of us have pondered why bad things happen to good people. It's especially difficult when we lose a loved one or experience loss of any kind.

We need to be careful in these moments to remember the truth that God loves us and His heart breaks with ours. He will never abandon or forsake us.

When we hold on to the grief, we can get lost in the loss, and the pain can become unbearable. However, we need to give it to God so that we don't suffer alone. He can do the impossible and turn even our worst situations for good.

He brings beauty from the ashes and loves you much more than you can ever understand.

# REDEEMED

## IDENTITY LIES:

- God doesn't love me.

- God doesn't care about my loss.

- God has abandoned me.

## THE TRUTH:

*Romans 8:38–39—"For I am convinced that neither death, nor life, nor angels, nor principalities, nor present things, nor future things, nor powers, nor height, nor depth, nor any other creature will be able to separate us from the love of God in Christ Jesus."*

*Matthew 5:4—"Blessed are they who morn, for they will be comforted."*

*Revelation 21:4—"He will wipe every tear from their eyes, and there shall be no more death or mourning, wailing or pain, [for] the old order has passed away."*

*Psalm 139:7—"Where can I go from your spirit? From your presence, where can I flee?"*

*Isaiah 43:2—"When you pass through waters, I will be with you; through rivers, you shall not be swept away. When you walk through fire, you shall not be burned, nor will flames consume you."*

# EMPOWERED

## PICKING UP THE PIECES

Are you ready to release your pain and grief to the Lord? Can you give it to Him and hear Him say, "I am with you, and I never left you. I cried with you, and I didn't desire these terrible things to happen to you. But I will bring good from it and beauty from the ashes. I will help you turn your pain into your passion. I will help you help others, and no matter what the fire is in your life that nearly took it, I will give you a new fire—the fire of love, the fire of truth, the fire of light, the fire of goodness, and the fire of redemption."

What trials or tragedies have happened in your life that have made you question God's love for you?

____________________________________________________________

____________________________________________________________

____________________________________________________________

________________________________________

________________________________________

________________________________________

________________________________________

________________________________________

________________________________________

Have you ever prayed, "God, where were you? Do you love me? Why did you let this happen?" What was that moment like?

________________________________________

________________________________________

________________________________________

________________________________________

________________________________________

________________________________________

________________________________________

What are some blessings God has given you throughout your life? Challenge yourself to fill each line!

________________________________________

_______________________________________

_______________________________________

_______________________________________

_______________________________________

_______________________________________

_______________________________________

Review the scriptures in "The Truth" section again. What do they mean to you?

_______________________________________

_______________________________________

_______________________________________

_______________________________________

_______________________________________

_______________________________________

# PRAYER

*Dear Lord, I'm so sorry for the times I've blamed you for all the bad things that have happened to me. Although you don't need forgiveness, I forgive you for allowing me to be in these terrible situations and release the pain I've been carrying to you. I want to be made new in you. I open my heart to receive your love, truth, and the fire of your Holy Spirit. Jesus, I surrender myself to you. Jesus, I trust in you. Amen.*

## CHAPTER 4

# LOSS

## RESTORED

God hears our prayers and answers them in His own way that is higher than ours.

When things go differently than we planned or expected, we might think He didn't hear us or that He has abandoned us. But actually, it's in our deepest darkness that He is closer than we could ever imagine—He is with us always, whether we feel like He is or not!

Also, when terrible things happen to us, we have the choice to draw closer to God or pull away from Him. However, when we pull away, fear enters in and we can't see His light.

Make sure to stay connected with Him through prayer during these times and trust that He will heal you and get you through the suffering.

# REDEEMED

## IDENTITY LIES:

- I'm all alone.

- God doesn't hear my prayers.

## THE TRUTH:

*Joshua 1:9—"I command you: be strong and steadfast! Do not fear nor be dismayed, for the LORD, your God, is with you wherever you go."*

*John 14:18—"I will not leave you orphans; I will come to you."*

*1 John 5:14-15—"And we have this confidence in him, that if we ask anything according to his will, he hears us. And if we know that he hears us in regard to whatever we ask, we know that what we have asked him for is ours."*

*Jeremiah 29:12—"When you call me, and come and pray to me, I will listen to you."*

*Luke 11: 9—"And I tell you, ask and you will receive; seek and you will find; knock and the door will be opened to you. For everyone who asks, receives; and the one who seeks, finds; and to the one who knocks, the door will be opened."*

*Isaiah 65:24—"Before they call, I will answer; while they are yet speaking, I will hear."*

# EMPOWERED

## PICKING UP THE PIECES

Have you ever lost someone and been stuck in the "whys"? *Why, Lord? Why now? Why this way?* Picture Jesus with you in that moment, crying with you and holding you in His arms. Hear Him say, "I am with you, and I will make all things new. I love you and will never leave you."

When have you asked for something in prayer and not received it? What was it? How did you feel when you did not receive what you asked for?

______________________________________________

______________________________________________

______________________________________________

______________________________________________

______________________________________________

_______________________________________________

_______________________________________________

Here on Earth, sometimes bad things happen in our lives, but God is always able to create something good from those circumstances. Think back to a negative event in your life. Did any good eventually come from it? Dig deep!

_______________________________________________

_______________________________________________

_______________________________________________

_______________________________________________

_______________________________________________

_______________________________________________

God knows what is best for us. He wants to help us live in true happiness. Sometimes, our prayers can sound more like a wish list. Remember that prayer is a conversation and a call to humble yourself to recognize and act on God's will. Can you think of a time when your prayer sounded like a wish list? How could you reword that prayer to allow for God's will, timing, and wisdom in your life?

_______________________________________________

_______________________________________________

_______________________________________________

25

# PRAYER

*Lord Jesus, you say that faith the size of a mustard seed can move a mountain. Please increase my faith and help me to keep my eyes fixed on you. Please comfort me in my afflictions and heal my memories so that no matter what has happened in the past, I can see that you are always with me and will never leave me. Thank you for bringing beauty from the ashes. Amen.*

## CHAPTER 5

# ABANDONMENT AND REJECTION

## RESTORED

God sees us even when we feel unseen by others, and He never wants us to lose hope. We need to be careful not to let other people's reactions and actions toward us bring us down.

Many times, the hurtful things people say and do to us come from their own place of woundedness. While it's not okay, we can't let it seep into our hearts and mold our identity. We need to give it to God and know that what He says about us is what matters most.

Also, to escape pain, you need to be careful to not hide behind a mask and try to become someone else. You are enough and made worthy in Christ and He sees you and loves you just the way you are! Your life is so valuable, that's why there's such an attack against it. Don't give up . . . brighter days are ahead.

Bottom line—God has a plan for your life and the world needs YOU!

# REDEEMED

## IDENTITY LIES:

- I'm invisible.
- My life has no purpose.

## THE TRUTH:

*Psalm 33:18—"Behold, the eye of the LORD is upon those who fear him, upon those who count on his mercy."*

*Job 34:21—"For his eyes are upon our ways, and all our steps he sees."*

*Psalm 139:1–2—"LORD, you have probed me, you know me: you know when I sit and stand; you understand my thoughts from afar."*

*Proverbs 19:21—"Many are the plans of the human heart, but it is the decision of the LORD that endures."*

*Jeremiah 29:11—"For I know well the plans I have in mind for you—oracle of the LORD—plans for your welfare and not for woe, so as to give you a future of hope."*

# EMPOWERED

We all have moments where we don't understand God's love and purpose for us. Have you ever felt lost and invisible? In these moments, it's important that you turn to the Truth and hear what God has to say.

Open your heart and ask the questions, "Lord, do you love me? Lord, do you see me? Lord, do you have a plan for my life?"

And hear Him say: "I am here, and I am near. No darkness and nothing you've ever done can keep me from you. Nothing can keep me from loving you. Nothing can keep me from living in you when you turn your life to me and invite me in. Come follow me, and I will tell you who you are. Come follow me, and I will restore your hope. Come follow me, and I will give you a future."

## PICKING UP THE PIECES

Was there a time in your life when you felt lost? What were the circumstances?

______________________________________________________

______________________________________________________

_______________________________________

_______________________________________

_______________________________________

_______________________________________

Have you ever felt like you have no idea who you are, where you are going, or how things could ever get better? Describe what happened.

_______________________________________

_______________________________________

_______________________________________

_______________________________________

_______________________________________

_______________________________________

Have you ever wondered, *Does anyone see me? Do I really exist?* How have you bought into the devil's lies?

_______________________________________

_______________________________________

_______________________________________

_______________________________________

_______________________________________

Pick a Scripture above that touches your heart and write it here. Try to memorize it and use it to combat the lies when they pop up.

_______________________________________________________________________

31

_______________________________________________________________________

_______________________________________________________________________

_______________________________________________________________________

_______________________________________________________________________

_______________________________________________________________________

# PRAYER

*Lord Jesus, I choose to open my heart to receive your love and truth. Please heal my mind, heart, body, and soul in any way that is needed. By your grace, may I always value my life and the lives of others. Please forgive me for the times that I haven't. Please help me to trust and believe in your plan for my life. Please help me to stop hiding behind things and start living fully alive as the person you created me to be. Please fill me with hope and truth and restore my life's purpose. Amen.*

## CHAPTER 6

# FEAR AND SHAME

## RESTORED

We all have done things we regret and wish we could take back. However, holding on to the shame and embarrassment becomes a roadblock to moving forward. The Gospel reminds us that in Christ we are made new!

While others can hurt and sting us with their words, God's opinion of us is what truly matters. And there's nothing we've ever done that He can't forgive—we just need to turn back to Him.

The enemy will try to get us to focus on our past mistakes, but God will remind us of our purpose and give us the strength to move forward. And when we surrender to Him, His light begins to shine through us to lead others to their own encounters with Him.

It's time for you to release the pain of your past so He can flood you with His love. You are a new creation in Christ—believe it!

# REDEEMED

## IDENTITY LIES:

- I'm bad.
- I don't belong.

## THE TRUTH:

*Genesis 1:27—"God created mankind in his image; in the image of God he created them; male and female he created them."*

*1 Timothy 4:4—"For everything created by God is good, and nothing is to be rejected when received with thanksgiving."*

*Ephesians 5:8—"For you were once darkness, but now you are light in the Lord. Live as children of light."*

*1 John 4:4—"You belong to God, children, and you have conquered them, for the one who is in you is greater than the one who is in the world."*

*Psalm 100:3—"Know that the LORD is God, he made us, we belong to him, we are his people, the flock he shepherds."*

# EMPOWERED

## PICKING UP THE PIECES

Think about the things others have said about you that have hurt you and stuck to your heart. Surrender them to Jesus who knows your pain and the truth about you. Even if you did something wrong, know that He is a God of mercy and forgiveness. He loves you!

You are only defined by who God says you are—His beloved child in whom He is well pleased.

Have you ever done something that you regret and wish you could take it back? What was it?

_______________________________________________

_______________________________________________

_______________________________________________

_______________________________________________

_______________________________________________

_______________________________________________

Has anyone ever bullied you or said/done something to hurt you? What happened and how did you feel?

__________________________________________________

__________________________________________________

__________________________________________________

__________________________________________________

__________________________________________________

__________________________________________________

Have you ever bullied someone else because of your own insecurities? What happened and why do you think you did that?

__________________________________________________

__________________________________________________

__________________________________________________

__________________________________________________

__________________________________________________

Have you ever joined in on the laughter when someone was being torn down? If so, write a letter to God expressing your heartfelt desire to be forgiven.

__________________________________________________

__________________________________________________

37

# PRAYER

*Lord Jesus, I forgive others for anything negative that has ever been said about me or has been done to me. I ask you to fill me with your truth and help me to see myself as you see me. I love you and thank you. Amen.*

## CHAPTER 7

# FINDING PURPOSE

## RESTORED

God gave us all different gifts and personalities to make this world a more beautiful place! As Saint John Paul II said, "You are unique and unrepeatable!" When we remember this and stop comparing ourselves to others, we have a sense of belonging. The joy that comes from being who we are created to be is contagious.

Discovery of our gifts and talents is part of the glue that the Master of our pieces uses to put us back together. God doesn't make mistakes—He makes Masterpieces. And where and how we become alive is an indicator of our life's purpose.

Be open to hearing Him and believing in His plan for you because He wants to lavish gifts on you, not take them away. Then, He wants you to use the gifts He has given you to bring Him glory.

# REDEEMED

## IDENTITY LIES:

- I'm not talented.

- God would never use someone like me.

## THE TRUTH:

*1 Corinthians 12:7—"To each individual the manifestation of the Spirit is given for some benefit."*

*1 Peter 4:10—"As each one has received a gift, use it to serve one another as good stewards of God's varied grace."*

*Matthew 5:16—"Just so, your light must shine before others, that they may see your good deeds and glorify your heavenly Father."*

*Isaiah 62:3—"You shall be a glorious crown in the hand of the Lord, a royal diadem in the hand of your God."*

*Proverbs 23:18—"For you will surely have a future, and your hope will not be cut off."*

# EMPOWERED

## PICKING UP THE PIECES

Spend some time in quiet reflection and ask the Lord to bring to mind the gifts you have and how they can be used to serve Him. Even in your home, workplace, and encounters with others, you can become a light in someone else's darkness.

What are some funny and good memories from your past that help remind you who you are and reveal part of God's plan for you?

_______________________________________________

_______________________________________________

_______________________________________________

_______________________________________________

_______________________________________________

_______________________________________________

What talents, gifts, and graces has God given you to share with others to bring them joy? Maybe you know how to play an instrument, or you know how to sing or draw. Perhaps you play a sport well and haven't played in years. Maybe you're a writer, and God is calling you to share your story. Whatever it is, acknowledge your gift and see how you can use it to bring God's love to others. List below some talents and gifts the Lord has given you.

______________________________________________

______________________________________________

______________________________________________

______________________________________________

______________________________________________

How can you put these gifts into action? Write three steps you can take to use them to bring God glory.

______________________________________________

______________________________________________

______________________________________________

______________________________________________

______________________________________________

______________________________________________

______________________________________________

# PRAYER

*Lord Jesus, thank you for the gifts and talents you have given me. Please help me to know them and use them to bring you glory. Help me to remember funny memories from my past that uncover glimpses of who I am in You. Amen.*

## CHAPTER 8

# NEW BEGINNINGS

## RESTORED

When we don't take time to pray, it will be difficult to hear God speak. He longs for us to spend time in silence to be alone with Him.

One of the best prayers we can make is to just have an honest conversation and pour our hearts out about what's going on and then listen for His response. He will always guide us to go in the right direction and His answers will come with peace. Then He will ignite our hearts to follow in His ways.

The prodigal son's story comes to mind—how God is always waiting for our return regardless of what we've done. We think we know what's best, mess up, exhaust our resources, and then are afraid to go back to God with our failures. However, he's so happy with our homecoming that He wants to throw us a party. That's one of the most surprising things about God—His love is constant and never fails. He never stops looking for us when we're lost and rejoices at our return. He always wants to re-establish our identity.

Our authority over the lies in the world and the lies in our hearts is in Him. He IS the Truth. However, we need to read the Bible and know His Word if we want to see the truth of who we are.

In His Word, you will discover that you are loved, chosen, forgiven, healed, redeemed, and created for a purpose. And once you believe you are who He says you are and He is who He says He is, you will find your true joy. God is always ready for your return!

# REDEEMED

## IDENTITY LIES:

- God would never speak to me.
- I don't know how to pray.

## THE TRUTH:

*Job 33:14—"For God does speak, once, even twice, though you do not see it."*

*Hebrews 4:12—"Indeed, the word of God is living and effective, sharper than any two-edged sword, penetrating even between soul and spirit, joints and marrow, and able to discern reflections and thoughts of the heart."*

*Jeremiah 33:3—"Call to me, and I will answer you; I will tell you great things beyond the reach of your knowledge."*

*Matthew 21:22—"Whatever you ask for in prayer with faith, you will receive."*

*Matthew 6:9-10—"This is how you are to pray, Our Father in heaven, hallowed be your name, your kingdom come, your will be done, on earth as in heaven."*

# EMPOWERED

## PICKING UP THE PIECES

What is your earliest experience of God that you can remember? Write about this or a time when you felt His presence in your life.

_______________________________________________

_______________________________________________

_______________________________________________

---

---

---

---

What changes did you make after this experience?

---

---

---

---

---

---

Did you keep up your prayer and relationship with God? If so, how? If not, why?

---

---

---

---

---

---

---

# PRAYER

*Lord Jesus, help me to be kind and loving to everyone in my life. Please help me to not leave others out and instead to be more inviting to them. Please help me to encounter you and to be on fire for the things you are on fire for. May the flame in my heart remain on fire and never burn out. Amen.*

# WORTHLESSNESS AND UNWORTHINESS

## RESTORED

It's better to not be in a relationship at all than to be in a bad one just because we fear being alone. And the right relationships will not drag us down but rather will encourage us to be who we are called to be. They will lead us closer to God.

May you never let anyone else define you and realize you are made worthy in Christ. When you trust Him and let go of what's not good for you, He will give you something so much better than you could ever imagine.

# REDEEMED

## IDENTITY LIES:

- I'm worthless.
- It's better to be in a bad relationship than to be alone.

## THE TRUTH:

*Luke 12:6-7—"Are not five sparrows sold for two small coins? Yet not one of them has escaped the notice of God. Even the hairs of your head have all been counted. Do not be afraid. You are worth more than many sparrows."*

*Isaiah 43:4—"Because you are precious in my eyes and honored, and I love you, I give people in return for you and nations in exchange for your life."*

*Isaiah 43:1—"But now, thus says the LORD, who created you, Jacob, and formed you, Israel: 'Do not fear, for I have redeemed you; I have called you by name: you are mine.'"*

*John 3:16—"For God so loved the world that he gave his only Son, so that everyone who believes in him might not perish but might have eternal life."*

*1 Corinthians 15:33—"Do not be led astray: 'Bad company corrupts good morals.'"*

# EMPOWERED

## PICKING UP THE PIECES

Have you ever been stuck in an unhealthy relationship and felt like it was the best you could do? What did it feel like?

---

---

---

---

---

Has anyone ever said something to you that made you feel like you couldn't leave a relationship? What was said or done that made you think this?

---

---

---

---

---

_______________________________________________

_______________________________________________

Are you afraid of being alone? Why?

_______________________________________________

_______________________________________________

_______________________________________________

_______________________________________________

_______________________________________________

Are there any relationships you need to surrender to God? Name them and explain why you need to let go.

_______________________________________________

_______________________________________________

_______________________________________________

_______________________________________________

_______________________________________________

_______________________________________________

Did anyone from your past come to mind as you read this chapter— someone that you may need to forgive and pray for?

55

# PRAYER

*Lord Jesus, please forgive me for any time that I have used another as an object and didn't see them as a person. Please guide my relationships and put people in my life who will value me and love me for who I am. Help me to know that you live in me and that I am eternally loved. Amen.*

# BETRAYAL

## RESTORED

Good friends are hard to find. Many people are selfish and put their needs above others. We need to seek friendships that bring us closer to God and ask for the grace to forgive those who have hurt us. It's not easy, but it's the only choice that will set us free.

The enemy loves when we hold a grudge and don't forgive because it's an open door for him to keep us in the hurts of our past. It can make us relive the pain over and over again.

We need to make a simple act of the will and say, "Jesus, this happened, but I choose to forgive and transfer the offense to you to deal with." This sets us free and releases the situation to Him, as each of us will be held accountable for everything we say or do.

Since we are made in the image of God and God is love, an offense against love is an offense against God. And while we are all prone to selfishness, it's through a relationship with Christ that we can begin to become more like Him. We can learn to love more selflessly—denying our desires for the good of another.

Let us ask God to give us the grace and strength not to turn inward but to turn outward. Let us beg Him for healthy relationships and good people to come into our lives—people who help restore our identity, not take it away. And may we forgive all those that have hurt us whether they meant to or not.

# REDEEMED

## IDENTITY LIES:

- I'm unprotected.
- I can't forgive.

## THE TRUTH:

*Psalm 23:4—"Even though I walk through the valley of the shadow of death, I will fear no evil, for you are with me; your rod and your staff comfort me."*

*Psalm 121:1–2—"I raise my eyes toward the mountains. From whence shall come my help? My help comes from the LORD, the maker of heaven and earth."*

*Psalm 91:1–2—"You who dwell in the shelter of the Most High, who abide in the shade of the Almighty, say to the LORD, 'My refuge and fortress, my God in whom I trust.'"*

*Matthew 6:14—"If you forgive others their transgressions, your heavenly Father will forgive you."*

*Luke 23:34—"Then Jesus said, 'Father, forgive them, they know not what they do."*

# EMPOWERED

## PICKING UP THE PIECES

Has someone been selfish and put their needs ahead of yours, to the point of compromising you and possibly harming you?

_______________________________________________

_______________________________________________

_______________________________________________

_______________________________________________

_________________________________________

_________________________________________

_________________________________________

Have you ever done that to someone else?

_________________________________________

_________________________________________

_________________________________________

_________________________________________

_________________________________________

_________________________________________

Do you need to forgive someone who once violated you? Are you ready to surrender the hurt to God? Share your heart with the Lord and let Him take your pain.

_________________________________________

_________________________________________

_________________________________________

_________________________________________

_________________________________________

_________________________________________

# PRAYER

*Lord Jesus, please help me to not be selfish and to be available to help others. Would you please grace me with friends that I can trust and who desire my good? I freely choose to forgive others for the times they were selfish and hurt me. By your grace, I forgive anyone who has ever violated me and know that justice is yours. I surrender the situation to you. Amen.*

## CHAPTER 11

# MOMENT OF TRUTH

## RESTORED

We all have made mistakes, but there is nothing God won't forgive when we repent and turn back to Him.

Sometimes we just need a little push and honesty from someone we trust—like someone to throw us into the confessional or drag us to church to realize that God is with us and never leaves us. He forgives and forgets once we bring our sins to Him. And the forgiveness of sin is a big deal. If we don't accept that, it's as if Jesus died for no reason. The entire point is that He loves us so much that He emptied Himself out on the cross for us—to restore, redeem, and empower us to be His disciples.

When He looks at you, He doesn't just see the broken pieces; He sees the whole picture. He knows the beauty of what can happen when you are reconciled with His truth and is delighted with your return. He sees the Masterpiece you were created to be.

# REDEEMED

## IDENTITY LIES:

- God will never forgive me.
- I'm too far gone.

## THE TRUTH:

*1 John 1:9—"If we acknowledge our sins, he is faithful and just and will forgive our sins and cleanse us from every wrongdoing."*

*Acts 3:19—"Repent, therefore, and be converted, that your sins may be wiped away."*

*Matthew 16:19—"I will give you the keys to the kingdom of heaven. Whatever you bind on earth shall be bound in heaven; and whatever you loose on earth shall be loosed in heaven."*

*Psalm 51:9—"Cleanse me with hyssop, that I may be pure; wash me, and I will be whiter than snow."*

*Matthew 9:12–13—"He heard this and said, 'Those who are well do not need a physician, but the sick do. Go and learn the meaning of the words, "I desire mercy, not sacrifice." I did not come to call the righteous but sinners.'"*

*2 Corinthians 3:17—"Now the Lord is the Spirit, and where the Spirit of the Lord is, there is freedom."*

# EMPOWERED

## PICKING UP THE PIECES

Who are you surrounding yourself with? What are the qualities you like most and least about them? What direction are they taking you in?

_______________________________________________

_______________________________________________

_______________________________________________

_______________________________________________

_______________________________________________

_______________________________________________

Who are the foundation stones in your life? Who is being Christ to you when you are in the darkness?

---

---

---

---

---

---

Who do you see struggling right now that needs an extra push? Who needs the freedom of knowing that they are loved just as they are and that nothing they've ever done could keep God away—that they're not tarnished or damaged goods?

---

---

---

---

---

---

How can you become the light and bring hope to others? Think of three things you can do to help them—send a message, say a prayer, etc.

# PRAYER

*Lord Jesus, thank you for the people in my life that lead by good example and encourage me. Help me to run the race toward you. Thank you for never giving up on me and for giving me a push when I need it through the hands of another. Amen.*

# BROKEN DREAMS

## RESTORED

We are often attacked by the people we least expect and sometimes we need to walk away from something we really wanted because it's not a safe situation to be in. Regardless of anything that's ever been done to us, we are made new in Christ.

Also, when we look back, we can observe that many times, we have been hurt in the very areas that reveal our giftings and callings. This is because the enemy will do whatever he can to try to get us to give up. He's terrified of the difference we can make in the world when we use what God has given us and walk in authority as children of God.

By reviewing your past, you may start to see glimpses into God's plan for your life and how the enemy tried to get you off the path and derail you. That said, nothing and no one can stop God's will for you when you turn to Him and trust!

# REDEEMED

## IDENTITY LIES:

- I'm tarnished.

- I'm dirty.

- Abuse is acceptable.

## THE TRUTH:

*2 Corinthians 5:17—"So whoever is in Christ is a new creation: the old things have passed away; behold, new things have come."*

*Revelation 21:5—"The one who sat on the throne said, 'Behold, I make all things new.' Then he said, 'Write these words down, for they are trustworthy and true.'"*

*Matthew 12:36—"I tell you, on the day of judgment people will render an account for every careless word they speak."*

*John 10:10—"A thief comes only to steal and slaughter and destroy; I came so that they might have life and have it more abundantly."*

*1 Corinthians 3:17—"If anyone destroys God's temple, God will destroy that person; for the temple of God, which you are, is holy."*

*Mark 9:42—"Whoever causes one of these little ones who believe (in me) to sin, it would be better for him if a great millstone were put around his neck and he were thrown into the sea."*

# EMPOWERED

## PICKING UP THE PIECES

Take time to watch videos of you from when you were growing up. Do you see any talents or patterns of behavior that may give a glimpse of your calling?

Have you ever had a broken dream? What happened?

________________________________

________________________________

________________________________

________________________________

________________________________

Has something terrible ever happened to you that you forgot about for a period of time or have hidden from others? What was it?  How did hiding your pain affect you and your relationship with others?

__________________________________________________

__________________________________________________

__________________________________________________

__________________________________________________

__________________________________________________

__________________________________________________

Where might shame be hiding in your heart?

__________________________________________________

__________________________________________________

__________________________________________________

__________________________________________________

__________________________________________________

__________________________________________________

Describe a time when you put on a mask to cover the pain.

---

---

---

---

---

Are you ready to face the pain and be set free? Are you prepared to let God restore your heart and dreams? Share how you are feeling by writing a letter to God below about your desire to let go and ask Him to heal you.

---

---

---

---

---

---

---

---

---

# PRAYER

*Lord Jesus, please heal the deep wounds in my heart that others have inflicted on me by seeing me as an object of use and not as a person. Please forgive me for using others in my past as well. Please heal me and help me to help others by turning my pain into my passion for setting captives free. Amen.*

## CHAPTER 13

# FAITHFUL WITNESSES

## RESTORED

We all long to belong and be in the Father's house, and our homes and hearts should be reflections of His love.

Venerable Father Patrick Peyton said, "A family that prays together stays together." When God blesses us with people that show us what love really looks like, it's such a gift. We can learn the truth through them and follow their example to be a light in the world.

We all feel unloved at times, but the moments where we experience true love or witness it in this life are like small glimpses into heaven.

# REDEEMED

## IDENTITY LIES:

- I don't know what love looks like.

- I'm not blessed.

## THE TRUTH:

*1 Corinthians 13:4–8—"Love is patient, love is kind. It is not jealous, [love] is not pompous, it is not inflated, it is not rude, it does not seek its own interests, it is not quick-tempered, it does not brood over injury, it does not rejoice over wrongdoing but rejoices with the truth. It bears all things, believes all things, hopes all things, endures all things. Love never fails."*

*Matthew 13:43—"Then the righteous will shine like the sun in the kingdom of their Father. Whoever has ears ought to hear."*

*Numbers 6:25–26—"The LORD bless you and keep you! The LORD let his face shine upon you, and be gracious to you! The LORD look upon you kindly and give you peace!"*

*Deuteronomy 7:9—"Know then, that the Lord, your God, is God: the faithful God who keeps covenant mercy to the thousandth generation toward those who love him and keep his commandments."*

*Ephesians 1:3—"Blessed be the God and Father of our Lord Jesus Christ, who has blessed us in Christ with every spiritual blessing in the heavens."*

# EMPOWERED

## PICKING UP THE PIECES

When things look dark, we need to focus on the light and the blessings that God has already given us. Consider documenting the date and how God blesses you in the Appendix located in the back of this workbook. Refer to this list in times of need.

God always comes through and it's important to focus on good and positive memories when we have experienced His love.

Who in your life has supported you when others haven't? How have they supported you? What did they say or do that left an impression on you and has impacted the way that you live?

_______________________________________________

_______________________________________________

______________________________

______________________________

______________________________

______________________________

______________________________

Who has been a good role model of the faith for you?

______________________________

______________________________

______________________________

______________________________

______________________________

______________________________

If you aren't married yet, have you prayed for a godly spouse? If you are married, are you praying with your spouse? If you are in religious life, are you praying in the community with your whole heart?

______________________________

______________________________

______________________________

______________________________

______________________________

# PRAYER

*Lord Jesus, help me remember the people in my life who have been positive examples of your love and mercy. May I cling to you in my time of need and trust that you have something beautiful planned and will never leave me despite my current circumstances. Lord, you know my needs. Please guide and provide. Amen.*

## CHAPTER 14

# INADEQUACY AND INSECURITY

## RESTORED

God has a purpose for each of us, and when we pursue Him, we will begin to see that purpose more clearly. It may take time, but the opportunities will show up, and He will equip us with what we need.

Also, we can't let the negative things others say about us stick to our hearts. Most people aren't in communion with the Lord, or they may say things thinking they are helping us when they don't understand God's plan for us. They can't see what He can see. They don't know what He knows. We need to learn to take every thought captive and make it obedient to Christ.

We need to remember that an invisible battle surrounds us, and the enemy's goal is to keep us from using our gifts to help others. The enemy will bombard us with lies that cause us to doubt what we are capable of. And if he can keep us down for the count, then we won't fulfill our mission in life and he wins.

However, this very fight also reveals God's purpose for us as we are often attacked the hardest when we are close to a major breakthrough. When we persevere and don't believe the enemy's lies, we will begin to see God's hand throughout the circumstances in our lives. He begins to open doors—that no one can shut!

We can't give up on the dreams and the deep desires that He places in our hearts—trust is key. They will come to fruition in His perfect timing.

God loves you and you have His spark within. It's a spark that no one can take away. The fire within you that has the power to ignite sparks in many people's hearts if you just let it.

# REDEEMED

## IDENTITY LIES:

- I'm not gifted.
- If someone says something negative about me, it must be true.

## THE TRUTH:

*Romans 11:29—"For the gifts and the call of God are irrevocable."*

*Psalm 23:1—"The LORD is my shepherd; there is nothing I lack."*

*James 1:17—"Every perfect gift is from above, coming down from the Father of lights, with whom there is no alteration or shadow caused by change."*

*Ephesians 6:12—"For our struggle is not with flesh and blood but with the principalities, with the powers, with the world rulers of this present darkness, with the evil spirits in the heavens."*

*Proverbs 4:23—"With all vigilance guard your heart, for in it are the sources of life."*

# EMPOWERED

## PICKING UP THE PIECES

Where might your gifting and calling be that the enemy doesn't want you to fulfill because of all the people you can help?

_______________________________________________

_______________________________________________

_______________________________________________

_______________________________________________

_______________________________________________

What hurtful things have others said that you need to give to Jesus? What is the truth?

_______________________________________________

_______________________________________________

_______________________________________________

_______________________________________________

_______________________________________________

_______________________________________________

What are some nice things others have said about you that maybe you didn't believe?

_______________________________________________

_______________________________________________

_______________________________________________

_______________________________________________

_______________________________________________

_______________________________________________

# PRAYER

*Lord Jesus, please go into my places of woundedness and heal me. Speak truth into my heart and open my eyes to see the mission you have for me. Help me to see the gifts you've given me so that I can fulfill your plan for my life. Amen.*

## CHAPTER 15

---

# DOUBT AND FEAR

## RESTORED

The more we dwell on a perceived imperfection, the more we draw attention to it. However, when we are alive in who we are created to be and are comfortable with our bodies, others can see us more clearly and focus on us as a person.

Preoccupation with ourselves takes us out of the present moment. If we are worried about someone noticing something we think is wrong with us, then we will not be fully present to the person right in front of us.

Dwelling on these things also causes interior pain and anxiety. However, when we release them to God, we can live in freedom. Then we can focus on what we're called to do and live with joy in our hearts. Inadequacy gets replaced with the truth that we are each unique and "enough."

While it's okay to wear makeup and dress nice, you can't begin to obsess about these things or let them become your idols. Are you putting on a mask to hide behind, or are you accentuating the real "you" in freedom? We are called not to conceal but to reveal.

There is freedom in surrender and accepting the truth of who you are in Christ. That is where true beauty begins because no amount of makeup can make a soul shine!

# REDEEMED

## IDENTITY LIES:

- I'm not beautiful.
- I need to impress others.

## THE TRUTH:

*Song of Songs 4:7—"You are beautiful in every way, my friend, there is no flaw in you!"*

*Psalm 34:6—"Look to him and be radiant, and your faces may not blush for shame."*

*1 Peter 3:3–4—"Your adornment should not be an external one: braiding the hair, wearing gold jewelry, or dressing in fine clothes, but rather the hidden character of the heart, expressed in the imperishable beauty of a gentle and calm disposition, which is precious in the sight of God."*

*Proverbs 31:30—"Charm is deceptive and beauty fleeting; the woman who fears the LORD is to be praised."*

*Proverbs 31:25—"She is clothed with strength and dignity, and laughs at the days to come."*

# EMPOWERED

## PICKING UP THE PIECES

How do you define beauty?

_______________________________________________

_______________________________________________

_______________________________________________

_______________________________________________

_______________________________________________

_______________________________________________

What do you find beautiful in others?

__________________________________________________

__________________________________________________

__________________________________________________

__________________________________________________

__________________________________________________

__________________________________________________

Has anyone ever said something that changed how you thought about your self-image in a negative way? How did you respond? What lies did you believe?

__________________________________________________

__________________________________________________

__________________________________________________

__________________________________________________

__________________________________________________

Are you ready to give the lies to God and let His truth in? Are you ready to get rid of the pieces of your false self and replace them with your true self? Write a note to God about how you are feeling right now about your beauty and worth.

_______________________________________________

_______________________________________________

_______________________________________________

_______________________________________________

_______________________________________________

_______________________________________________

_______________________________________________

_______________________________________________

_______________________________________________

_______________________________________________

# PRAYER

*Dear Jesus, please help reveal to me how beautiful I am in you. Show me the areas that I am struggling with and please go into those places and heal my heart and mind. Help me to live freely and fully in the body I've been given, and may I give thanks and praise for it. Amen.*

## CHAPTER 16

---

# FAILURE

## RESTORED

It's not the house that makes the home, it's the love that exists within its walls that counts. And sometimes focusing on views of the created can actually obscure our view of the Creator if we put them above Him.

We also need to be careful to discern relationships before we get too deeply into them. When we seek God's will and are prayerful, He will guide us to healthy ones.

Remember that no matter what you've done or what mess you've gotten yourself into, it's never too late for redemption. When you let go and "let God," He brings good out of everything and you receive back a hundredfold. He heals and resurrects your broken heart and His plan will always triumph.

# REDEEMED

## IDENTITY LIES:

- If I get more things, I will be happy.

- I messed up and I'm stuck.

## THE TRUTH:

*1 Timothy 6:17—"Tell the rich in the present age not to be proud and not to rely on so uncertain a thing as wealth but rather on God, who richly provides us with all things for our enjoyment."*

*Psalm 73:26—"Though my flesh and my heart fail, God is the rock of my heart, my portion forever."*

*Psalm 23:3—"He restores my soul. He guides me along right paths for the sake of his name."*

*Isaiah 54:17—"Every weapon fashioned against you shall fail; every tongue that brings you to trial you shall prove false. This is the lot of the servants of the LORD, their vindication from me—oracle of the LORD."*

*Matthew 19:26—"Jesus looked at them and said, "For human beings this is impossible, but for God all things are possible."*

# EMPOWERED

## PICKING UP THE PIECES

Do you discern relationships before getting into them and ask God what He desires for you?

What went well in past romantic relationships?

What didn't go well in past romantic relationships?

_______________________________________________

_______________________________________________

_______________________________________________

_______________________________________________

_______________________________________________

_______________________________________________

What could you work on in regard to romantic relationships past and/ or present?

_______________________________________________

_______________________________________________

_______________________________________________

_______________________________________________

_______________________________________________

_______________________________________________

How can you use the wounds of your past to bring healing to others?

_______________________________________________

_______________________________________________

_______________________________________________

# PRAYER

*Lord Jesus, please help me to know what relationships are good for me, and please be in the middle of all of them. Please help heal my heart from anyone who has hurt me. Jesus, please take the wheel of my life and steer me in the right direction. Amen.*

# PAIN AND SUFFERING

## RESTORED

We all suffer moments of severe pain, but let us keep our eyes on the gift of life. Many times, we are asking God for a miracle but forget we are the miracle!

We were born for a reason, and although we may not have had a perfect family life or childhood, God can turn all things into blessings. While we can't escape suffering in this life, we can remember that we are not alone in these moments and keep hope alive.

God will never abandon you and is the closest to you in your most excruciating affliction.

# REDEEMED

## IDENTITY LIES:

- Things are hopeless.

- The pain is more than I can handle.

## THE TRUTH:

*Romans 15:13—"May the God of hope fill you with all joy and peace in believing, so that you may abound in hope by the power of the Holy Spirit."*

*Romans 12:12—"Rejoice in hope, endure in affliction, persevere in prayer."*

*Hebrews 11:1—"Faith is the realization of what is hoped for and evidence of things not seen."*

*Isaiah 41:10—"Do not fear: I am with you; do not be anxious: I am your God. I will strengthen you, I will help you, I will uphold you with my victorious right hand."*

*Philippians 4:6-7—"Have no anxiety at all, but in everything, by prayer and petition, with thanksgiving, make your requests known to God. Then the peace of God that surpasses all understanding will guard your hearts and minds in Christ Jesus."*

# EMPOWERED

## PICKING UP THE PIECES

Can you look back at a time when you experienced extreme pain, whether emotionally, mentally, spiritually, or physically, and then out of nowhere, peace came over you? Maybe a friend called just in time or perhaps you were aware of the presence of a loved one that had passed away? Describe that time.

______________________________________________________

______________________________________________________

______________________________________________________

______________________________________________________

______________________________________________________

Were you ever in so much pain—emotional, mental, spiritual, or physical—that you felt like you had no one to help you or hear you but God? Describe that time.

______________________________________________________

______________________________________________________

___________________________________________

___________________________________________

___________________________________________

___________________________________________

___________________________________________

Where do you need a new beginning in your life right now? Write a prayer to God and ask Him to fill you with hope regarding your new beginning. Look forward to what He has planned for you.

___________________________________________

___________________________________________

___________________________________________

___________________________________________

___________________________________________

___________________________________________

# PRAYER

*Heavenly Father, you are the source of all life. You gave each of us life for a reason, and I am here for a purpose. Thank you for the miracle of my life. May I live it in you, with you, and for you! Amen.*

# CHAPTER 18

# DECEPTION

## RESTORED

We live in a world that points out our flaws and increases our insecurities in order to try to sell us something we don't even need.

Also, many things try to hide under the guise of good, but darkness must always come to the light. For example, our culture tries to persuade us that naughty is nice and bad is good. But that's not possible because we are made in the image of God, who is love—and truth and love are inseparable. Anything that is not true will never fulfill us.

When we are living a lie and not doing what we are created for or are misusing God's gifts and leading people in the wrong direction, it will never feel right.

Truth is life, while lies and misleading others leads to death—naughty can never be nice!

# REDEEMED

## IDENTITY LIES:

- I'm helpless.

- I can use something bad for good.

- The things of the world will fill the holes in my heart.

## THE TRUTH:

*Timothy 1:7—"For God did not give us a spirit of cowardice but rather of power and love and self-control."*

*1 John 5:4—"For whoever is begotten by God conquers the world. And the victory that conquers the world is our faith."*

*1 John 2:17—"Yet the world and its enticement are passing away. But whoever does the will of God remains forever."*

*Matthew 6:19—"Do not store up for yourselves treasures on earth, where moth and decay destroy, and thieves break in and steal."*

*Matthew 16:26—"What profit would there be for one to gain the whole world and forfeit his life? Or what can one give in exchange for his life?"*

# EMPOWERED

## PICKING UP THE PIECES

What perceived physical imperfections have you struggled with?

_______________________________________________

_______________________________________________

_______________________________________________

_______________________________________________

_______________________________________________

How much time and energy are you spending trying to fix these imperfections or worrying about them? How can you give your imperfections to God?

_______________________________________________

_______________________________________________

_______________________________________________

_______________________________________________

_______________________

_______________________

_______________________

Where might God be speaking to you in your life's decisions in order to direct you to the right path?

_______________________

_______________________

_______________________

_______________________

_______________________

_______________________

Where or how do you find peace? List some places or activities that have brought you peace in the past. Name your "happy place."

_______________________

_______________________

_______________________

_______________________

_______________________

_______________________

# PRAYER

*Dear Jesus, please help me to know your will and give me the grace and strength to do it. Help me to not be insecure about my perceived imperfections but rather surrender them to you. Please help me to know my true worth and beauty and that I am not alone. Please redeem my past mistakes and lead me in the right direction. Amen.*

## CHAPTER 19

# IDENTITY LOSS AND TRAUMA

## RESTORED

When anyone abuses us, whether it be physically, mentally, emotionally, or spiritually, it's NOT okay! We need to get to a safe place and let God heal us.

While God doesn't desire any suffering for us, He loves us so much that He gives us the ability to make choices. Because of this, sometimes others decide to hurt us. But we can't remain stuck in our pain; we must go to Jesus with all our strength and He will help us to turn our pain into our passion.

Don't forget, He is closest to you at your rock-bottom moments—when you are in desperate need of Him. It's in these times that you should unite your suffering with His as His burden is light. He wants to raise you above the hurts because He loves you and He will heal your memories when you let Him. Even your fiercest, darkest pains of the past can be used to help others.

Always remember your identity in Christ is your backbone. He is your foundation and the strength of your entire being.

# REDEEMED

## IDENTITY LIES:

- Violence is okay.
- I'm too broken and my pain is wasted.

## THE TRUTH:

*Matthew 7:12—"Do to others whatever you would have them do to you. This is the law and the prophets."*

*Matthew 7:20—"So by their fruits you will know them."*

*Proverbs 22:24—"Do not be friendly with hotheads, nor associate with the wrathful."*

*Romans 12:19—"Beloved, do not look for revenge but leave room for the wrath; for it is written, 'Vengeance is mine, I will repay,' says the Lord."*

*Romans 12:21—"Do not be conquered by evil but conquer evil with good."*

*Matthew 11:28-30—"Come to me, all you who labor and are burdened, and I will give you rest."*

*Psalm 56:9—"My wanderings you have noted; are my tears not stored in your flask, recorded in your book?"*

*Romans 5:3–4—"Not only that, but we even boast of our afflictions, knowing that affliction produces endurance, and endurance, proven character, and proven character, hope."*

*Psalm 34:19—"The LORD is close to the brokenhearted, saves those whose spirit is crushed."*

*Psalm 147:2–3—"The LORD rebuilds Jerusalem, and gathers the dispersed of Israel, healing the brokenhearted, and binding up their wounds."*

# EMPOWERED

## PICKING UP THE PIECES

Describe a time in which you felt paralyzed emotionally, spiritually, mentally, or physically.

_______________________________________________

_______________________________________________

_______________________________________________

_______________________________________________

_______________________________________________

_______________________________________________

Who has hurt you that you need to forgive?

_______________________________________________

_______________________________________________

_______________________________________________

_______________________________________________

_______________________________________________

What are some of the most broken pieces of your life that have come up while reading this book—pieces that you need God to heal?

__________________________________________________

__________________________________________________

__________________________________________________

__________________________________________________

__________________________________________________

What pain and trials do you need God's grace with right now?

__________________________________________________

__________________________________________________

__________________________________________________

__________________________________________________

__________________________________________________

# PRAYER

*Dear Jesus, in this world, people hurt us in so many ways. I give you my will to forgive them and trust in you for justice. Please give me the strength and grace to get through these dark times. Amen.*

## CHAPTER 20

# LOVE OF OUR FATHER

## RESTORED

When we turn our lives back to God, miracles begin to happen! He loves us much more than we could ever imagine and forgives and forgets our sins when we repent and trust in Him.

As Saint John Paul II said, "We are not the sum of our weaknesses and failures. We are the sum of the Father's love for us and our real capacity to become the image of His Son Jesus."

Our Father, "Abba," not only hears our cries but also delivers us from all evil. He is omnipotent and stronger than anything that tries to come against us—nothing stands above God and nothing and no one could ever keep us away from His love.

The only power the enemy has is the power that we give him. We need to learn to ignore him and pray to God our Father who has a tender and merciful heart for those in need. He will fight our battles for us!

Our Father can move mountains, and if He hasn't answered your prayers yet, it's because He has something better. He can see what you can't, and what you think is good may not be His will or it might not be the right timing. However, God's ways and timing are always perfect.

# REDEEMED

## IDENTITY LIES:

- I don't need to read the Bible.

- I don't need to repent or confess my sins.

- The enemy is stronger than God.

## THE TRUTH:

*Joshua 1:8—"Do not let this book of the law depart from your lips. Recite it by day and by night, that you may carefully observe all that is written in it; then you will attain your goal; then you will succeed."*

*Proverbs 28:13—"Those who conceal their sins do not prosper, but those who confess and forsake them obtain mercy."*

*Psalm 32:1—"Blessed is the one whose fault is removed, whose sin is forgiven."*

*Luke 7:47–48—"So I tell you, her many sins have been forgiven; hence, she has shown great love. But the one to whom little is forgiven, loves little. He said to her, 'Your sins are forgiven.'"*

*James 4:7—"So submit yourselves to God. Resist the devil, and he will flee from you."*

*Micah 7:8—"Do not rejoice over me, my enemy! Though I have fallen, I will arise; though I sit in darkness, the LORD is my light."*

*Romans 8:15—"For you did not receive a spirit of slavery to fall back into fear, but you received a spirit of adoption, through which we cry, 'Abba, Father!'"*

*Deuteronomy 20:4—"For it is the LORD, your God, who goes with you to fight for you against your enemies and give you victory."*

*Psalm 27:1—"The LORD is my light and my salvation; whom should I fear? The LORD is my life's refuge; of whom should I be afraid?"*

*Lamentations 3:57–58—"You drew near on the day I called you; you said, 'Do not fear!' You pleaded my case, Lord, you redeemed my life."*

*Philippians 2:10—"That at the name of Jesus every knee should bend, of those in heaven and on earth and under the earth."*

*John 8:36—"So if the son frees you, then you will truly be free."*

# EMPOWERED

## PICKING UP THE PIECES

What is your relationship like with God our Father? How do you envision Him? How do you envision Jesus?

___________________________________________

___________________________________________

___________________________________________

___________________________________________

___________________________________________

___________________________________________

When was the last time you sought forgiveness for your sins? Have you truly repented from past sin or are you just going through the motions?

_______________________________________________

_______________________________________________

_______________________________________________

_______________________________________________

_______________________________________________

_______________________________________________

Do you believe that you are truly forgiven, or have you been stuck in shame and regret?

_______________________________________________

_______________________________________________

_______________________________________________

_______________________________________________

_______________________________________________

_______________________________________________

# PRAYER

*Abba, Father, help me to know your love and trust in you. Protect me and deliver me from all evil. Please help me to rest in the power of your love and mercy. Thank you for always desiring to give me what is best for me even when I don't realize it. Amen.*

# CHAPTER 21

# ADORATION

## RESTORED

When we read the Bible, we encounter the truth of what God thinks about us.

We need to spend a lot of time in silence to allow this truth to sink in and let God rebuild our identity in Him. Being restored to who we truly are and being firmly rooted in it doesn't happen overnight. However, after much time in silence, it's easier to hear the small whisper in our hearts and the words of love that the Lord is hungry to speak to us. It could be like a thought in the heart, or maybe a song or Scripture comes to mind.

Sometimes He speaks through someone else who affirms us in our identity, or we get an email or text that answers our questions. His voice takes many forms, but He will answer us, and His answer will be consistent. It will also come with peace and joy that heals our hearts.

Spending time in intimate prayer with God or in Adoration of the Blessed Sacrament also increases the beauty of our souls and it will radiate through us. Because God is love and we receive His love through prayer, it increases the love in our own hearts, thus making us more beautiful. As Saint Augustine said, "Love IS the beauty of the soul."

# REDEEMED

## IDENTITY LIES:

- I could never reflect God's glory.
- My thoughts define me.
- I don't know how to find God or feel His presence.

## THE TRUTH:

*Galatians 2:20—"Yet I live, no longer I, but Christ lives in me; insofar as I now live in the flesh, I live by faith in the Son of God who has loved me and given himself up for me."*

*Romans 12:2—"Do not conform yourselves to this age but be transformed by the renewal of your mind, that you may discern what is the will of God, what is good and pleasing and perfect."*

*Psalm 145:18—"The LORD is near to all who call upon him, to all who call upon him in truth."*

*Jeremiah 29:13—"When you look for me, you will find me. Yes, when you seek me with all your heart."*

*Psalm 46:11–12—"Be still and know that I am God! I am exalted among the nations, exalted on the earth." The LORD of hosts is with us; our stronghold is the God of Jacob."*

*John 6:56—"Whoever eats my flesh and drinks my blood remains in me and I in him."*

*Matthew 5:8—"Blessed are the clean of heart, for they will see God."*

# EMPOWERED

## PICKING UP THE PIECES

Are you ready to know the truth and be set free? Plan a time to go to Adoration or spend time in quiet reflection and bring a pen and paper with you. Ask the Lord to bring to light the lies that you are holding in your heart and give them to Him. Also, take time when you look in the mirror to see

Jesus in your eyes and remember that He lives in you and is with you. He will restore, redeem, and empower you to be you!

Have you ever asked the Lord who He says you are? What was the response? If not, ask Him and write what comes to mind.

_________________________________________________________________

_________________________________________________________________

_________________________________________________________________

_________________________________________________________________

_________________________________________________________________

Ask the Lord to bring to light the lies that you are holding in your heart and write them down.

_________________________________________________________________

_________________________________________________________________

_________________________________________________________________

_________________________________________________________________

_________________________________________________________________

_________________________________________________________________

Are you ready to spend time with Him in silence and be persistent in prayer? Do you believe He will answer you? Write a personal prayer surrendering the lies that have come to mind and accepting the truth.

# PRAYER

*Lord Jesus, let me decrease so that you can increase. May your love shine through me onto others so that your beauty may be revealed. Help me to know the truth of who I am and to be deeply rooted in it so that I get my identity from you—not from what the world tells me. Please give me the grace to live in the world but not be of it. I love you and know that you love me more. Amen.*

## CHAPTER 22

# COMMUNITY

## RESTORED

While solitude can be satisfying, God created us to be in community, and it's essential to spend time together with others who are journeying with God. When we realize the beauty of community and are not trying to do everything by ourselves, we will be amazed at what can be accomplished. Together we can do much . . . alone, so little.

Also, the more illumined our souls become, the more we see that we are incredibly weak on our own, and that all the good in us is God Himself. But He makes us strong and uses us despite our weaknesses, as long as we turn to Him for strength. Hence, the spiritual life is full of paradoxes—in our weakness, we are made strong, and in losing our lives, we gain them.

# REDEEMED

## IDENTITY LIES:

- I could never be religious.

- Others will think I'm crazy if I try to be holy.

- If people are against me, I must be bad.

- I don't need community; I can do everything by myself.

## THE TRUTH:

*Luke 9:24—"For whoever wishes to save his life will lose it, but whoever loses his life for my sake will save it."*

*Proverbs 20:24—"Our steps are from the LORD; how, then, can mortals understand their way?"*

*Matthew 5:10—"Blessed are they who are persecuted for the sake of righteousness, for theirs is the kingdom of heaven."*

*John 15:18–19—"If the world hates you, realize that it hated me first. If you belonged to the world, the world would love its own; but because you do not belong to the world, and I have chosen you out of the world, the world hates you."*

*2 Corinthians 12:10—"Therefore, I am content with weaknesses, insults, hardships, persecutions, and constraints, for the sake of Christ; for when I am weak, then I am strong."*

*Matthew 18:19— "Again, [amen,] I say to you, if two of you agree on earth about anything for which they are to pray, it shall be granted to them by my heavenly Father."*

*Romans 12:4–5—"For as in one body we have many parts, and all the parts do not have the same function, so we, though many, are one body in Christ and individually parts of one another."*

# EMPOWERED

## PICKING UP THE PIECES

How is God calling you to be involved in His Church? Are there any religious lay orders that God may be calling you to? Have you ever discerned a call to religious life?

________________________________________

________________________________________

________________________________________

________________________________________

________________________________________

________________________________________________

________________________________________________

When have doubt and fear prevented you from doing something God was calling you to?

________________________________________________

________________________________________________

________________________________________________

________________________________________________

________________________________________________

Have you sensed a tugging in your heart to attend any community or church events? Have you looked at the church bulletin lately for activities in the parish that God may be calling you to help serve or participate in?

________________________________________________

________________________________________________

________________________________________________

________________________________________________

________________________________________________

Do you have a favorite saint? Who is it and why? Remember to ask them to intercede for you daily and know you are never alone on this journey.

# PRAYER

*Lord Jesus, help me to see your hand in all things. Please help me to understand my calling in life and to have clarity on the path to holiness. Saint Teresa of Avila, pray for us! Amen.*

## CHAPTER 23

# USING YOUR GIFTS

## RESTORED

It can be scary to make a life change, but when we use our gifts for God's glory, the decision will come with peace, joy, and passion—nothing else will ever satisfy.

Sometimes we need to close a door to something that's not God's desire for us, and He will open a new one in His time. We don't need to understand how it will happen but just trust that our life and happiness are a big deal to Him.

When our wills are aligned with His, we will have the energy and excitement to move in the direction He is leading. And as long as we are living righteous lives, our inner compass (The Holy Spirit) will always guide us in which way to go.

God will give us the grace, strength, and everything else we need to succeed in our missions. Seeking Him, trusting in Him, and remaining firm in our choices are key.

# REDEEMED

## IDENTITY LIES:

- I don't know what direction to go.
- The sacrifice will be too great.

## THE TRUTH:

*Psalm 32:8—"I will instruct you and show you the way you should walk, give you counsel with my eye upon you."*

*Isaiah 30:21—"And your ears shall hear a word behind you: 'This is the way; walk in it,' when you would turn to the right or the left."*

*Proverbs 3:5–6—"Trust in the LORD with all your heart, on your own intelligence do not rely; In all your ways be mindful of him, and he will make straight your paths."*

*Matthew 13:45–46—"Again, the kingdom of heaven is like a merchant searching for fine pearls. When he finds a pearl of great price, he goes and sells all that he has and buys it."*

*Job 42:2—"I know that you can do all things, and that no purpose of yours can be hindered."*

# EMPOWERED

## PICKING UP THE PIECES

Have you ever been a part of something you knew God didn't want you to do anymore? What was it? How did you get out of it? How did you feel after you made the change?

_______________________________________________

_______________________________________________

_______________________________________________

_______________________________________________

_______________________________________________

_______________________________________________

Are you currently discerning God's will in an area of your life? What is the situation and what do you feel like His will could be? Do you have peace with this decision?

_______________________________________________

_______________________________________________

_______________________________________________

_______________________________________________

_______________________________________________

_______________________________________________

Have you experienced opposition in a choice you made to serve God? What happened?

_______________________________________________

_______________________________________________

_______________________________________________

_______________________________________________

_______________________________________________

_______________________________________________

# PRAYER

*Lord Jesus, please help me know your will for my life. Please guide me, strengthen me, and provide for me. Thank you for always wanting the best for me and having such amazing plans for my life. I love you. Amen.*

## CHAPTER 24

# EVANGELISM

## RESTORED

Surrendering to God isn't easy, but His plans are always bigger and better than we could ever imagine. We need to walk in blind faith knowing He will guide us and give us everything that is needed for His plan to come to fruition.

When we feel something so deeply in our hearts, we can't go by what others say; we need to do it anyway and work according to our strengths.

Remember when God calls you to do something, nothing and no one can stop it other than yourself. The enemy will do his best to get you to turn around. He will try to convince you that you aren't good enough or experienced enough. However, you are made in the image of God, and God IS, so you ARE. You are enough, and He doesn't put deep desires in your heart that He doesn't want to fulfill.

God wants you to trust Him with abandon, and if something isn't meant to be, then it won't happen. However, you won't know unless you try. Even when things seem impossible, you just have to trust the Lord and go for it. The results are in His hands!

# REDEEMED

## IDENTITY LIES:

- I don't have what it takes.
- I don't know if or how God's plan will happen.

## THE TRUTH:

*Philippians 4:13—"I have the strength for everything through him who empowers me."*

*Romans 10:11—"For the scripture says, "No one who believes in him will be put to shame."*

*2 Corinthians 12:9—"But he said to me, 'My grace is sufficient for you, for power is made perfect in weakness.' I will rather boast most gladly of my weaknesses, in order that the power of Christ may dwell with me."*

*Proverbs 16:3—"Entrust your works to the LORD, and your plans will succeed."*

*Habakkuk 2:3—"For the vision is a witness for the appointed time, a testimony to the end; it will not disappoint. If it delays, wait for it, it will surely come, it will not be late."*

*Isaiah 46:10–11—"At the beginning I declare the outcome; from of old, things not yet done. I say that my plan shall stand, I accomplish my every desire. I summon from the east a bird of prey, from a distant land, one to carry out my plan. Yes, I have spoken, I will accomplish it; I have planned it, and I will do it."*

*Psalm 37:5—"Commit your way to the LORD; trust in him and he will act."*

*Mark 11:24—"Therefore I tell you, all that you ask for in prayer, believe that you will receive it and it shall be yours."*

# EMPOWERED

## PICKING UP THE PIECES

Have you ever felt called to something but were scared to do it? What was it? How did you handle it?

_______________________________________________

_______________________________________________

_______________________________________________

_______________________________________________

_______________________________________________

_______________________________________________

Have you ever had someone else tell you that you couldn't do something even though you knew it felt right inside? What was it? How did you respond to the doubters?

_______________________________________________

_______________________________________________

_______________________________________________

_______________________________________________

_______________________________________________

_______________________________________________

Have you ever waited to hear back from someone, and it seemed like forever, and you began to fear for the worst? How did it turn out?

_____________________________________________

145

_____________________________________________

_____________________________________________

_____________________________________________

_____________________________________________

_____________________________________________

In tough situations, have you remembered to ask God to guide you and all those involved to do His will? Share a time you invited God into a discernment and how things turned out or a time when you didn't invite Him and realize now that you should have.

_____________________________________________

_____________________________________________

_____________________________________________

_____________________________________________

_____________________________________________

_____________________________________________

# PRAYER

*Lord Jesus, please help me to trust in you and follow the prompts of the Holy Spirit. Please open the doors that need to be opened in my life and close the doors that need to be closed. You know what is best for me. Help me to hear your voice and persevere even when others try to make me doubt. Please take away any fear of the future as I freely choose to place it in your loving hands. Amen.*

## CHAPTER 25

# USING YOUR HURTS

### RESTORED

While God never wills for bad things to happen to us, He allows things to happen because of other people's free will and the fact that we live in a fallen world.

However, He loves us deeply and promises to bring good out of everything. He brings beauty from the ashes and allows us to use our wounds and experiences to bring healing to others.

We're all called to be wounded healers, and it's love that heals. Being a wounded healer isn't about worthiness—it's about mission. It's about being the hands and feet of Jesus.

Once you allow His love to heal and fill your wounds, you can become more sympathetic toward others who are hurting. You will share in His compassion for what they are going through and become a light in their darkness. And as the Lord puts your broken pieces back together, His light begins to shine through the mosaic Masterpiece He has created.

# REDEEMED

## IDENTITY LIE:

- I'm too broken to help others.

## THE TRUTH:

*Isaiah 53:5—"But he was pierced for our sins, crushed for our iniquity. He bore the punishment that makes us whole, by his wounds we were healed."*

*Mark 16:17–18—"These signs will accompany those who believe: in my name they will drive out demons, they will speak new languages. They will pick up serpents [with their hands], and if they drink any deadly thing, it will not harm them. They will lay hands on the sick, and they will recover."*

*Mark 9:23—"Jesus said to him, 'If you can! Everything is possible to one who has faith.'"*

*Psalm 37:23-24—"The valiant one whose steps are guided by the LORD, who will delight in his way, may stumble, but he will never fall, for the Lord holds his hand."*

*Romans 8:28—"We know that all things work for good for those who love God, who are called according to his purpose."*

# EMPOWERED

## PICKING UP THE PIECES

Spend time in prayer, asking the Lord to reveal your wounds and allowing Him to enter into your woundedness to fill you with His truth and love. Take time to see what gifts, talents, and graces you've been given. Let God decide how to use your gifts and talents to bring healing to others. Follow the prompts of the Holy Spirit daily and go where He tells you to go. Be God's light in the world!

What are some of the biggest wounds from your past?

_________________________________________________

_________________________________________________

_______________________________________________

_______________________________________________

_______________________________________________

_______________________________________________

Have you healed? If so, how? If not, what do you think you could do to begin on a path of healing?

_______________________________________________

_______________________________________________

_______________________________________________

_______________________________________________

_______________________________________________

_______________________________________________

How can you use all of your past, all of your wounds, all of those things that kept you away from Christ to become a wounded healer?

_______________________________________________

_______________________________________________

_______________________________________________

_______________________________________________

_______________________________________________

_______________________________________________

# PRAYER

*Lord Jesus, please heal me in any way that is needed so that I can bring your healing love to others and serve you. Thank you for speaking to me through others and circumstances. Help me to be a wounded healer who brings your light into the world. Amen.*

## CHAPTER 26

---

# IDENTITY IN CHRIST

## RESTORED

It's important to go on retreats and take time out of our busy schedules to grow in our relationship with God. Also, hearing other people's testimonies at the retreats will help remind us that we're never alone in our suffering and that many people have been through similar things we can relate to.

You may have had experiences over the years that chipped away at your identity, and you may have even said your name with a question mark. But God our Father wants you to know who you really are and that you belong to Him. May you get to the point of being able to say your name with confidence in Him and stay rooted and grounded in His truth for good.

Also, never be afraid to share your story—remember, it's all for His glory!

# REDEEMED

## IDENTITY LIE:

- I don't know who I am.

## THE TRUTH:

*Jeremiah 1:5—"Before I formed you in the womb I knew you, before you were born I dedicated you, a prophet to the nations I appointed you."*

*Galatians 4:7—"So you are no longer a slave but a child, and if a child then also an heir, through God."*

*1 Peter 2:9—"But you are a chosen race, a royal priesthood, a holy nation, a people of his own, so that you may announce the praises of him who called you out of darkness into his wonderful light."*

*Ephesians 2:10—"For we are his handiwork, created in Christ Jesus for the good works that God has prepared in advance, that we should live in them."*

*1 Corinthians 13:12—"At present we see indistinctly, as in a mirror,*
*but then face to face. At present I know partially; then I shall know*
*fully, as I am fully known."*

# EMPOWERED

## PICKING UP THE PIECES

Consider starting a prayer wall in your home or putting together an album where you can put Scriptures that have touched your heart and photos of "God-incidences."

Have you ever had to get up in front of someone and say your name? How did you feel? Did you feel confident in knowing who you truly are?

______________________________________________

______________________________________________

______________________________________________

______________________________________________

______________________________________________

______________________________________________

Have you ever questioned who you are and why you're here? What happened that made you start thinking about that?

_______________________________________________

_______________________________________________

_______________________________________________

_______________________________________________

_______________________________________________

_______________________________________________

Are you able to see Christ in yourself and others? Give an example.

_______________________________________________

_______________________________________________

_______________________________________________

_______________________________________________

_______________________________________________

If you were to start a prayer wall in your home or a photo album with "God-incidences," what are some things you would include?

_______________________________________________

_______________________________________________

_______________________________________________

# PRAYER

*Lord Jesus, help me to know the true meaning of my name and to say it with confidence. Please help me to know my worth and to see you in others. May we all be united in your love and feel safe in your most Sacred heart. Amen.*

## CHAPTER 27

# LISTENING TO THE HOLY SPIRIT

## RESTORED

Saint Therese spent years trying to find her vocation and her calling. Even though she had become a nun and submitted her life to the Lord, it bothered her that she didn't know what her specific purpose was within her vocation. Finally, she figured it out one day and exclaimed, "At last, I have found my vocation. In the heart of the Church, I will be Love."

Like Saint Therese, our vocation is to love everyone, to see Christ in everyone, and to bring people to Him. We all have a story to share that can help others. And as you grow in your relationship with God, you will begin to follow His lead more easily. Just remember to ask Him every day to guide your steps and be open to who He puts in front of you.

# REDEEMED

## IDENTITY LIES:

- I don't know what my calling is, and I don't know what to do.
- God would never speak through me.

## THE TRUTH:

*John 13:34—"I give you a new commandment: love one another. As I have loved you, so you also should love one another."*

*2 Samuel 23:2—"The spirit of the LORD spoke through me; his word was on my tongue."*

*Isaiah 55:11—"So shall my word be that goes forth from my mouth; It shall not return to me empty, but shall do what pleases me, achieving the end for which I sent it."*

*Luke 12:12—"For the holy Spirit will teach you at that moment what you should say."*

*Matthew 10:20—"For it will not be you who speak but the Spirit of your Father speaking through you."*

# EMPOWERED

## PICKING UP THE PIECES

Begin now to take time to think about who you truly are. The Appendix at the back of this book has some words to help get you started. Circle the ones that you connect with the most.

Who are you? What is God calling you to do today? Where do you become most alive?

___________________________________________

___________________________________________

___________________________________________

___________________________________________

___________________________________________

___________________________________________

How can you be a witness to His mercy?

___________________________________________

___________________________________________

___________________________________________

___________________________________________

___________________________________________

How can you live out the vocation to love?

____________________________________

____________________________________

____________________________________

____________________________________

____________________________________

____________________________________

Who can you share His love with today?

____________________________________

____________________________________

____________________________________

____________________________________

____________________________________

____________________________________

What encounters and circumstances have you experienced that might help you understand your life's purpose better?

____________________________________

____________________________________

____________________________________

163

Using the Appendix, choose a few words that describe who you really are. Write them down below and refer to this list in times of doubt.

# PRAYER

*Spend five minutes in silence every day this week, asking The Lord, "Who am I? What is my calling?" and see what He says.*

## CHAPTER 28

# FREEDOM IN CHRIST

## RESTORED

It is normal to experience doubts, fears, and anxieties, but true freedom in Christ allows us to move forward despite how we feel. When we do this, we will be shocked and ecstatic at what God can accomplish through us. We need only to be obedient and trust.

Knowing the Scriptures is knowing the truth, which ultimately breaks our chains so we can live in freedom and be who God created us to be. Then we will also be able to speak life into the hearts of others—to set captives free.

The enemy will do his best to try to take away your voice because he knows the difference you can make in the world by speaking the truth. You need to be aware of his lies, recognize them, and reject them immediately.

God will never fail you and will always provide what you need. You need to trust in Him and be courageous. It's not about perfection—it's about participation.

# REDEEMED

## IDENTITY LIES:

- I can't make it through this difficult time.
- I won't know what to say.
- God won't provide.

## THE TRUTH:

*Isaiah 40:31—"They that hope in the LORD will renew their strength, they will soar on eagles' wings; they will run and not grow weary, walk and not grow faint."*

*Isaiah 41:13—"For I am the LORD, your God, who grasps your right hand; It is I who say to you, Do not fear, I will help you."*

*Galatians 5:1—"For freedom Christ set us free; so stand firm and do not submit again to the yoke of slavery."*

*Isaiah 61:1—"The spirit of the Lord GOD is upon me, because the LORD has anointed me; He has sent me to bring good news to the afflicted, to bind up the brokenhearted, to proclaim liberty to the captives, release to the prisoners."*

*Jeremiah 20:9—"I say I will not mention him, I will no longer speak in his name. But then it is as if fire is burning in my heart, imprisoned in my bones; I grow weary holding back, I cannot!"*

*Matthew 6:25–27—"Therefore I tell you, do not worry about your life, what you will eat [or drink], or about your body, what you will wear. Is not life more than food and the body more than clothing? Look at the birds in the sky: they do not sow or reap, they gather nothing into barns, yet your heavenly Father feeds them. Are not you more important than they? Can any of you by worrying add a single moment to your life-span?"*

*Matthew 6:33–34—"But seek first the kingdom (of God) and his righteousness, and all of these things will be given you besides. Do not worry about tomorrow; tomorrow will take care of itself."*

*Philippians 4:19—"My God will fully supply whatever you need, in accord with his glorious riches in Christ Jesus."*

*1 Kings 17:14—"For the LORD, the God of Israel, says: 'The jar of flour shall not go empty, nor the jug of oil run dry, until the day when the LORD sends rain upon the earth."*

# EMPOWERED

## PICKING UP THE PIECES

In what area of your life do you feel you are attacked the most? Why do you think that is?

_______________________________________

_______________________________________

_______________________________________

_______________________________________

_______________________________________

_______________________________________

What lies run through your mind that hold you back or make it difficult to use a gift to help others?

_______________________________________

_______________________________________

_______________________________________

How have you been dealing with doubts, fears, and lies? Have you noticed them? What is your reaction when they surface?

What Bible verses help you to overcome these falsehoods? Write down any that come to mind or ones that have struck your heart while using this workbook.

# PRAYER

*Lord Jesus, you are my healer. Please bring to light the lies that hold me back from serving you more deeply. Please set me free, and may your truth be deeply rooted in my heart. Help me to hear your small whisper telling me the truth of who I am and what I am capable of in you! Amen.*

## CHAPTER 29

# RESTORED DREAMS

### RESTORED

When we face our fears and move forward with God's will, we will eventually be able to step into the roles He intended for us all along. We just have to surrender and keep on going.

He levels the playing field and resurrects our dreams and the truth of who we are in Him. He then begins to place His dreams in our hearts—ones so much better than we could ever come up with on our own. And while surrendering to Divine Providence daily isn't easy, it allows God to work miracles in our lives.

What would it look like for you to open your heart and ask Him to place his dreams in it? Can you believe that God thinks you're good enough and that He can accomplish His mission in you? It's the truth—step out in faith to embrace it.

# REDEEMED

## IDENTITY LIES:

- God's plan won't come to fruition in my life.
- Other people can stop God's plan for me.

## THE TRUTH:

*Luke 1:45—"Blessed are you who believed that what was spoken to you by the Lord would be fulfilled."*

*Psalm 37:4—"Find your delight in the LORD who will give you your heart's desire."*

*Matthew 25:21—"His master said to him, 'Well done, my good and faithful servant. Since you were faithful in small matters, I will give you great responsibilities. Come, share your master's joy.'"*

*Ecclesiastes 3:14— "I recognized that whatever God does will endure forever; there is no adding to it, or taking from it. Thus has God done that he may be revered."*

*Luke 1:37—"For nothing will be impossible for God."*

*Acts 1:8—"But you will receive power when the holy Spirit comes upon you, and you will be my witnesses in Jerusalem, throughout Judea and Samaria, and to the ends of the earth."*

*Revelation 3:8—"I know your works (behold, I have left an open door before you, which no one can close)."*

*Psalm 33:11—"But the plan of the LORD stands forever, the designs of his heart through all generations."*

*Isaiah 14:27—"The LORD of hosts has planned; who can thwart him? His hand is stretched out who can turn it back?"*

# EMPOWERED

God's dreams are always so much bigger and better than we could ever imagine. He often uses our past, purifies it, and resurrects it when we surrender our lives to Him. He has the final say!

## PICKING UP THE PIECES

Do you have any broken dreams that you need God to heal or restore?

_______________________________________________________

_______________________________________________________

_______________________________

_______________________________

_______________________________

_______________________________

_______________________________

Have you ever asked Him to place His dream for you in your heart? If not, write a note to Him below asking Him to dream in your heart and to give you three next steps.

_______________________________

_______________________________

_______________________________

_______________________________

_______________________________

_______________________________

How have you responded to inspirations in the past, and what opportunities has the Lord put in your path that help reveal His will for you?

_______________________________

_______________________________

_______________________________

_______________________________

_______________________________

Do you realize that God is your defender and will help make your dreams come true? Make statements of affirmation and gratitude below trusting God with your dreams and life.

______________________________________________________

______________________________________________________

______________________________________________________

______________________________________________________

______________________________________________________

______________________________________________________

# PRAYER

*Heavenly Father, your dream for my life is so much bigger and better than anything I could ever think of on my own. Please place your dream for me in my heart and give me the grace and strength to follow through. Amen.*

## CHAPTER 30

# FEELING OTHERS' PAIN

## RESTORED

True discipleship will lead us to help others, and it is in giving that we receive.

We are all called to feed hungry hearts and become the face of God to others in need.

It's love alone that heals and to give love is to give life. We can breathe life into another by simply taking time to notice them, listen to them, and pray with them.

Are you taking the time to nourish and feed other people's hearts? Are you even aware of the hunger in your own?

# REDEEMED

## IDENTITY LIES:

- I don't need to help others or the poor.

- God wouldn't use me to heal.

- My prayers don't work.

- The Lord won't deliver me from my affliction.

## THE TRUTH:

*Galatians 5:14—"For the whole law is fulfilled in one statement, namely, 'You shall love your neighbor as yourself.'"*

*1 Corinthians 16:14—"Your every act should be done with love."*

*Hebrews 13:2—"Do not neglect hospitality, for through it some have unknowingly entertained angels."*

*James 5:16—"Therefore, confess your sins to one another and pray for one another, that you may be healed. The fervent prayer of a righteous person is very powerful."*

*Psalm 107:28—"In their distress they cried to the LORD, who brought them out of their peril."*

*Psalm 34:5—"I sought the LORD, and he answered me, delivered me from all my fears."*

# EMPOWERED

## PICKING UP THE PIECES

Read this quote once with your head and then a second and third time slowly with your heart. Then ponder these questions:

> *"Christ has no body but yours, no hands, no feet on earth but yours, yours are the eyes with which he looks with compassion on this world. Yours are the feet with which he walks to do good. Yours are the hands with which he blesses all the world."*
> —*Saint Teresa of Avila*

How can you help feed someone else's heart today? How can you become God's hands and feet in this lonely world?

__________________________________

__________________________________

__________________________________

__________________________________

__________________________________

Have you ever felt the Lord asking you to help another? What was your response? Were you afraid to help out? If so, what lie held you back?

_______________________________

_______________________________

_______________________________

_______________________________

_______________________________

_______________________________

Pick one of the Scriptures from "The Truth" section that stood out to you. What is the Lord saying to you?

_______________________________

_______________________________

_______________________________

_______________________________

_______________________________

_______________________________

# PRAYER

*Lord Jesus, help me to be your hands and feet in this world and become your face to others. May I see everyone with your compassion and tender heart, and may I be restored in your name. Please feed and heal my hungry heart. Amen.*

## CHAPTER 31

# HOPE AND RESURRECTION

## RESTORED

Things don't always look like what we thought they would. However, by living a life in Christ, we can start to see light in even the darkest of places. We must never forget the resurrection and that while our lives here are short, we are made for heaven.

We also need to remember that the enemy will tell us lies that go against the resurrection in our lives. He does this because he's terrified of what the world would look like if we all lived with a resurrection mentality.

Imagine if we realized that none of our problems were too big for God and that He will restore and redeem us. It's not that we won't suffer but that we can unite our crosses with His and allow Him to bring resurrection to our hearts. As Saint John Paul II said, "We are the Easter people and Alleluia is our song."

Are you experiencing the loss of something right now that you desperately need the Lord to bring back to life? What are you grieving over that is causing affliction? A broken relationship? A broken dream? The loss of a loved one? The loss of a job? Abandonment? Loneliness?

Whatever it is, realize that Jesus is grieving with you. His heart is stirred with love, and He's longing to bring you resurrection in that area.

# REDEEMED

## IDENTITY LIES:

- I'll never see my loved one again.
- Heaven doesn't exist.
- I don't know what to say.

## THE TRUTH:

*Hebrews 12:1—"Therefore, since we are surrounded by so great a cloud of witnesses, let us rid ourselves of every burden and sin that clings to us and persevere in running the race that lies before us."*

*John 11:25—"Jesus told her, 'I am the resurrection and the life; whoever believes in me, even if he dies, will live.'"*

*Daniel 12:3—"But those with insight shall shine brightly like the splendor of the firmament, And those who lead the many to justice shall be like the stars forever."*

*Philippians 3:20—"But our citizenship is in heaven, and from it we also await a savior, the Lord Jesus Christ."*

*Luke 23:43—"He replied to him, 'Amen, I say to you, today you will be with me in Paradise.'"*

*Jeremiah 1:9—"Then the LORD extended his hand and touched my mouth, saying to me, 'See, I place my words in your mouth!'"*

# EMPOWERED

## PICKING UP THE PIECES

Have you ever prayed for something that came true but didn't look like what you thought it would? What was it and what happened?

______________________________________

______________________________________

______________________________________

______________________________________

______________________________________

Have you ever lost someone you were very close to and questioned God about why they had to die or leave the way they did?

_____________________________________________________

_____________________________________________________

_____________________________________________________

_____________________________________________________

_____________________________________________________

How are you handling the trials and fires in your life? Are you turning away from God or toward Him?

_____________________________________________________

_____________________________________________________

_____________________________________________________

_____________________________________________________

_____________________________________________________

Recall some good memories of your loved ones who have passed. What can you learn from their lives?

# PRAYER

*Heavenly Father, you have my life planned down to my last breath. When tragedy strikes, it's difficult for me to see your loving hand. Please help me to know that you are with me and love me. I know when I get to heaven it will all make sense. Please help me with my grief and heal me in your merciful heart. Amen.*

## CHAPTER 32

# MOVING FORWARD

## RESTORED

Once the Lord begins to heal our lives, He calls us to heal others. With our eyes open, we will start to see the opportunities to help them and be more present.

God is the great "I AM." He is not stuck in the past or the future, as He is outside of space and time. He is with us always and is constantly trying to communicate with us, and He wants to use us to bring His love into the world.

The person right in front of us is our calling at the moment, and since we are judged on love, we need to evaluate how well we love. And this applies not just to the people that love us back, but also those who feel forgotten about and have no one to love them. Take it a step further: what about our enemies? How can we love the people who have hurt us?

It takes a hero's heart to forgive and love without expecting anything in return. But it's true that the more we give, the more we receive. As Saint John of the Cross said, "Put love, where there is no love, and find love."

Even if we don't feel love returned from the person we give it to, we will find God's sacrificial love inside of us. It's a supernatural, superhero kind of love that can only be accomplished through Love Himself.

We will then begin to walk not with human confidence, but with God confidence. We will no longer let the flames and fires in life consume us, but we will become the fire. We will be able to move forward and persevere knowing that all things are possible in Him and that He *IS* our strength. By His grace, we can make a difference in this world and leave a legacy of love—love that lives on forever!

Never forget that Jesus is the Master of your pieces. He and only He defines you. He will restore, redeem, and empower you to be who He's created you to be—so you can set the world on fire!

# REDEEMED

# THE TRUTH REIGNS!!!

# THE TRUTH:

*1 Corinthians 13:13—"So faith, hope, love remain, these three; but the greatest of these is love."*

*John 1:5—"The light shines in the darkness, and the darkness has not overcome it."*

*1 Corinthians 15:55—"Where, O death, is your victor? Where, O death, is your sting?"*

*Psalm 46:6—"God is in its midst; it shall not be shaken; God will help it at break of day."*

*Philippians 1:6—"I am confident of this, that the one who began a good work in you will continue to complete it until the day of Christ Jesus."*

*1 Corinthians 9:24—"Do you not know that the runners in the stadium all run in the race, but only one wins the prize? Run so as to win."*

*Luke 12:49—"I have come to set the earth on fire, and how I wish it were already blazing!"*

# EMPOWERED

## PICKING UP THE PIECES

- Focus on your good column. If you focus on who you are and what you are created for and choose to love other people, then you're not sinning.

- Your identity is in Christ, and you are who He says you are. The Bible tells you so.

- Above all, read and tell His story, and may your story become HIStory!

- Surrender to a daily relationship with Him. There is no other way to happiness.

- Be in conversation and communion with the Lord.

- Meditate on the Scriptures and let His Word sink into your heart.

---

# GOD'S LOVE NEVER FAILS, AND GOD'S LOVE NEVER DIES.

---

# PRAYER

*Lord Jesus, thank you for being the Master of my pieces. Thank you for the healing I've experienced already. I ask that you continue to heal my life. May I never forget who I am in you. Please continue to help me through the various trials and fires in life so that I don't get burned. May the fire of your love grow fervently in my heart. Thank you for dying to save me and for the plans that you have for my future. Jesus, I trust in you. Amen.*

# APPENDIX

## WHO AM I?

| | | |
|---|---|---|
| Beloved | Redeemed | Worthy |
| Protected | Healed | Encouraging |
| Prayer warrior | Free | Evangelist |
| Soldier for Christ | Part of a community | Cherished |
| Provided for | A believer | Gracious |
| Beautiful | Christian | Called |
| Prophet | Survivor | Special |
| Wounded Healer | Found | Fervent |
| Made new | Strengthened | Made in His image |
| Adopted | Hopeful | A reflection |
| Good friend | Strong | Sacred |
| Faith-filled | A gift | Sound-minded |
| Peaceful | A treasure | Strong |
| Inspiring | Holy | One of a Kind |
| Knowledgeable | Pure | Accepted |
| Confident | Forgiven | Royalty |
| Sweet | Giving | Clean |
| Blessed | Peacemaker | Sanctified |
| Honored | Merciful | New |
| Loveable | Disciple | Enough |
| Caring | Joyful | Fully Known |
| Compassionate | Brave | Renewed |
| Not alone | Spiritual mother | Hopeful |
| A good sister | Leader | A Delight |
| Intuitive | Smart | Adopted |
| Kind | Bold | Seen |
| Loving | Open | Victorious |
| Sensitive | Seeking Christ | Gifted |
| A child of God | Witness | Talented |
| Daughter | Unique | Alive |
| Child of light | Blossoming | Spirit-filled |
| Chosen | Focused | Planned |
| Favored | Courageous | His |
| Trusted | Virtuous | Masterpiece |
| Raised | Loving | Restored |
| Saved | Peacemaker | Redeemed |
| Delivered | Adventurous | Empowered |
| Graced | Trusting | Perfectly Loved |

# LIST OF BLESSINGS TO REMEMBER
# IN TIMES OF DARKNESS

DATE                              EVENT

_______________________________________________

_______________________________________________

_______________________________________________

_______________________________________________

_______________________________________________

_______________________________________________

_______________________________________________

_______________________________________________

_______________________________________________

_______________________________________________

_______________________________________________

# PUTTING THE PIECES OF YOUR STORY TOGETHER

What was your relationship like with God as a child?

_______________________________________________

_______________________________________________

_______________________________________________

_______________________________________________

As a teen?

_______________________________________________

_______________________________________________

_______________________________________________

_______________________________________________

As an adult?

_______________________________________________

_______________________________________________

_______________________________________________

_______________________________________________

Name three main broken pieces in your life.

______________________________________________

______________________________________________

______________________________________________

______________________________________________

Name a time God tried to shine light through your broken piece (for example, through circumstance, a Scripture, or another way).

______________________________________________

______________________________________________

______________________________________________

______________________________________________

Was there a turning point where you surrendered your life to the Lord? If so, what happened?

______________________________________________

______________________________________________

______________________________________________

______________________________________________

______________________________________________

What did you change in your life after that?

______________________________________

______________________________________

______________________________________

______________________________________

If you have not faced a turning point yet, what broken pieces has the Lord been bringing to mind? What steps can you make to allow Him to heal you so you can encounter His love more deeply—prayer, going to church, joining a Bible study, etc.?

______________________________________

______________________________________

______________________________________

______________________________________

What are your unique gifts and talents?

______________________________________

______________________________________

______________________________________

______________________________________

How may the Lord be calling you to help others?

______________________________________________

______________________________________________

______________________________________________

______________________________________________

______________________________________________

Be ready to share your story with someone in need. You never know who you can help. God is with us!

# YOUR STORY

Take what you wrote and put it all together.

# ABOUT THE AUTHOR

Joelle Maryn is an award-winning actress, international speaker, and TV host. In her past, she modeled for many national brands, was on a billboard in Times Square, and graced the covers of numerous books and publications.

Several years ago, Joelle had a miraculous conversion experience and now shares her message of God's healing love around the world. She also engages in faith-based, inspirational, and family-friendly films and TV shows to help lead others closer to Christ.

Joelle recently produced, co-wrote, and starred in the award-winning film *Fully Known*. And as host of Shalom World TV's *Beyond the Vision*, she has been blessed to interview many celebrities and public figures. In addition, Joelle has appeared on several international podcasts, radio broadcasts, and TV shows, including *The Journey Home* on EWTN.

When she's not on camera or at speaking engagements, Joelle's favorite things are walking on the beach, watching sunrises and sunsets, singing, dancing like no one is watching, and spending time with family, especially her beloved children.

You can learn more about her mission at www.JoelleMaryn.com.